41 MINUTES TO BE HAPPY

First published in 2022 in the French
language, originally under the title:
41 minutes pour être heureux by First
Éditions, an imprint of Edi8, Paris

Published in 2023 by Hardie Grant Books,
an imprint of Hardie Grant Publishing

Hardie Grant Books (London)
5th & 6th Floors
52–54 Southwark Street
London SE1 1UN

Hardie Grant Books (Melbourne)
Building 1, 658 Church Street
Richmond, Victoria 3121

hardiegrantbooks.com

British Library Cataloguing-in-Publication
Data. A catalogue record for this book is
available from the British Library.

41 Minutes to be Happy
ISBN: 978-1-78488-630-1

10 9 8 7 6 5 4 3 2 1

For the Edi8 edition:
Publisher: Aline Sibony
Editing: Lisa Marie
Proofreading: Judith Lévitan
Page layout and illustrations: La bonne
adresse

For the Hardie Grant edition:
Publishing Director: Kajal Mistry
Acting Publishing Director: Emma Hopkin
Senior Editor: Eila Purvis
Proofreader: Emma Bastow
Production Controller: Gary Hayes

Colour reproduction by p2d
Printed and bound in China by Leo Paper
Products Ltd.

MIX
Paper from
responsible sources
FSC™ C020056

GÉRAUD GUILLET

41 MINUTES TO BE HAPPY

– The 7 Pillars of Happiness –

Hardie Grant

BOOKS

CONTENTS

FOREWORD

———— The idea for this book was born following a humanitarian mission to the Philippines. While there, I was moved by the great zest for life of the Filipino people, despite their incredible hardship[1]. The contrast with our team of Western volunteers shook me. We, who seemed to have every reason to be happy, were all at sea, in an ocean of sadness and complaints – a far cry from the limitless joy of our hosts. On my return from the mission, I needed to understand why these people were so happy, while we were not. Above all, I wanted to discover how we too could attain this joyfulness that had made such an impression on me. After several years, this quest for happiness has finally come to an end.

To bring my work to fruition, I applied the methodology used for my first book, *L'Expérience TESK* (*The TESK Experience*), which has given thousands of people around the world the tools they need to give up smoking. The creation of this book required an analysis of the most advanced scientific studies on the notions of wellbeing and happiness. The writing of contemporary authors such as Tal Ben-Shahar, Frédéric Lenoir and Sonja Lyubomirsky have inspired it, as have the works of numerous philosophers who

have pondered over the universal subject of happiness.
A series of interviews with medical experts
(psychologists, psychiatrists and therapists) has also
allowed me to substantiate my words.

But it is mostly the testimonies of anonymous
contributors that have made this work what it is.
In particular, those of our elders. Why? Because their
collective memory constitutes a universal fund, more
precious than all the knowledge in the world.
Their wisdom and experience are unrivalled as fuel
for reflection on all kinds of subjects, beginning with
happiness. To benefit from this great wealth, which
can only be acquired with age, just one thing is
required of us: the willingness to listen.

This book is dedicated to our elders.

HAPPINESS IS . . . A DEEP-SEATED YEARNING SHARED BY ALL MEMBERS OF THE HUMAN FAMILY. IT SHOULD BE DENIED TO NO ONE AND AVAILABLE TO ALL.

– Ban Ki-moon –

INTRODUCTION

———— Over the past few years, happiness has become such a major preoccupation throughout the world that 20 March 2012 was designated International Day of Happiness[2]. Why such enthusiasm? Perhaps because 'happiness is ... a deep-seated yearning shared by all members of the human family. It should be denied to no one and available to all'[3], as proclaimed in 2014 by Ban Ki-moon, then Secretary-General of the UN. Or, above all, because approximately 280 million people in the world suffer from depression[4], an illness characterised by a profound feeling of melancholy that affects people of any income, nationality or social class. This book seeks to act as a defence against that sad reality, and it is my primary concern that it is effective. Using a simple and innovative approach, its ambition is to be useful to all; to those in search of happiness, those who wish to rediscover it, and those who do not want to lose it.

Each person who contributed to this work has their own idea of happiness. However, they all agreed on a common definition that approximates happiness to joy, the emotion that is most beautifully expressed in a child's laughter.

At the heart of this book, there is a conviction: that there are seven universal pillars that we can all rely on to seize life joyfully.

Drawing on exceptional lives, remarkable testimonies and numerous references to literature, philosophy and cinema, *41 Minutes to be Happy* aspires to a unique experience: a deep dive into the heart of a process that, page after page, will help you to identify the things that are stifling your happiness and those that are essential to it. At the end of the journey, you will be invited to navigate life through the lens of joy, leaning on those indestructible pillars that, in opposition to sadness and unhappiness, comprise **meaning**, **truth**, **strategy**, **love**, **body and mind**, **confidence** and **giving**.

NOTE

This book was conceived as an aid to those wishing to find, or rediscover, the path of happiness. It should not, under any circumstances, substitute the advice and care of a doctor or therapist, whom any person experiencing distress would be advised to consult.

RULES

'Obedience is the mother of success...'
Aeschylus

RULE #01

IF THIS IS YOUR FIRST READ
OF THE BOOK, YOU SHOULD READ
IT IN ONE GO*.

RULE #02

UNPLUG:
NO TELEPHONE,
NO TV AND NO INTERNET.

RULE #03

TAKE AS LONG AS YOU NEED
TO READ IT.

RULE #04

BEFORE STARTING TO READ,
FIND A NOTEPAD AND SOMETHING
TO WRITE WITH.

*Estimated reading time: 41 minutes.

ARE YOU READY?
LET'S GO!

MEANING

'If you want to live a happy life,
tie it to a goal...'

– Albert Einstein –

PAUL

Could you introduce yourself?

— My name is Paul; I'm English and I'm 81. I'm an engineer by training. I've spent my whole career in the automobile industry. I've been married to Rose for nearly 50 years. We live in the Dulwich area of London. Together we have three children, 14 grandchildren and eight great-grandchildren.

What is your definition of happiness?

— For me, happiness is first and foremost the love of those close to me. Not glory, nor power, nor even health, but love. And then motor racing, of course!

Are you happy today?

— I am the happiest of men. At my age, I try to make the most of each moment. I live each day of my life as though it were the last!

At which point in your life were you the happiest?
— On 3 May 1972. That's the day I met Rose. As soon
as I saw her, I knew that she was the love of my life.
Three months later, I asked her to marry me.

At which point in your life were you the most
unhappy?
— On 10 June 1964. That day, my best friend Brian and
I were returning from the wedding of a friend of
ours. On the road, in the middle of the night, a lorry
hit our car. The impact was hard, and the car didn't
survive. Brian was fine, but me, I lost the use of my
legs. Permanently. I was 27 years old.

What happened afterwards?
— In the months following the accident, I was lost. One
operation followed another: I suffered physically but
also psychologically. I didn't know what I was going
to do with my life. All my dreams had evaporated.
Nothing had any importance any more.

How did you overcome this?
— After a year, when I was still very depressed, my
father set me a challenge: to make a list of all the
things I wanted to achieve in my life, without
imposing any restrictions and without taking

my handicap into account. I rose to the challenge, initially to please him. I dug deep, and I came up with a list. Among my craziest 'dreams' were working in the automobile industry, climbing Mount Kilimanjaro, acting in a Shakespeare play on stage, starting a family and even one day driving a car again. Today, I have accomplished all these things.

What happened?

— As soon as I had written it, I couldn't stop thinking about that list, about all those dreams that were nagging at me. That's when I started to feel better. Those dreams, those challenges, brightened my daily life: they gave it meaning. My father had hit the mark. Little by little, I began to make all sorts of plans to bring what was sitting on that list to fruition. That's how I freed myself from my own unhappiness, to focus on everything that would pull me out of it.

Is realising our dreams the key to happiness?

— Yes and no. Of course, it's always nice to succeed in what you undertake, and there's no question that makes you happy. But what really counts, deep down, is giving meaning to your life. Setting yourself goals is one way of doing it. That makes us reflect on what really motivates us, and on what makes us happy.

What would you like to say to all those who want to be happy?

— Give meaning to your life – make your list! Don't let any obstacles stand in your way, and don't let anyone tell you what you want to hear! Listen only to your heart, then jump right in!

What should we say to those who don't achieve their goals?

— It doesn't matter! Don't be afraid; everyone fails. Nothing is set in stone. Your dreams will continue to evolve according to your encounters, your failures and your successes. I have never stopped adding dreams to my list. Deep down, what's important is not arriving at the end of the path but walking the right path, the one that 'grabs you by the guts'. You'll know that you're on the right path when you no longer want to look back.

NOW

List three achievements that you are proud of.

AFTER READING THE BOOK

*Make a list of ten things that you would like to accomplish
in your life.*

GIVING *MEANING* TO YOUR LIFE, FEEDING IT WITH GOALS, IS ESSENTIAL TO WALKING THE PATH OF HAPPINESS. BUT NO GOAL WILL HAVE VALUE IF IT IS NOT ROOTED IN *TRUTH*.

TRUTH

'The language of truth is simple.'
Seneca

MY FATHER THE HERO

———— When I was a child, I was fortunate to have been a very good student, excelling in virtually every subject. I had a particular gift for mathematics. My good grades were a source of pride for my father, who was a graduate of one of the top engineering schools in France ; they seemed to make him particularly happy. Throughout my childhood, I therefore strove to work hard, particularly in mathematics, and was rewarded by my father's joy at discovering my report card.

During my high-school years, things got complicated. While my heart leaned towards economics and literature, I felt a strong paternal pressure urging me to choose the sciences. Without much conviction, I went down the route of the science baccalaureate. That's when the problems really began. Instead of continuing to work like the model student I had been, I found that, without really understanding why, I was no longer putting the work in. Worse, I not only abandoned my studies; I also began to drift. Farewell the great engineering career dreamt of by my father; hello a course of study at a university whose few study hours and the lack of supervision appealled to me. In the end, everyone was disappointed: my father, of course, and especially me, directionless in my studies and not knowing what I wanted to do with my life.

It wasn't until a few years later, when I enrolled in a management school, that I rediscovered an appetite for studying. I became passionate about business strategy and, little by little, the joy of studying returned. It was only while working on this book that I truly understood what I had experienced during my time at high school: instead of embracing my love for the arts and economics, I tried to follow my father's direction rather than my own passions.

This anecdote has reminded me how imperative it is to remain true to one's convictions and to live according to one's truth, whatever the cost. Our happiness depends upon it.

FIGHT CLUB

Each individual is shaped by a number of characteristics, such as physical capabilities, political beliefs, artistic tastes and religious faith. All of these features, whether they be innate or acquired over time, forge our personality; they constitute our truth. According to many psychologists[6], the affirmation of our truth – or the affirmation of oneself – is an essential component of happiness[7]. Unfortunately, however, it is not always easy to affirm one's truth because as soon as this diverges from the norm, it often leads to rejection of our friends, of our family and even of society as a whole.

Millions of people experience rejection every day, from the most banal to the most serious. In these circumstances, it is tempting to deny our truth! This negation of self may allow us to avoid confrontation, but in the longer term, it inevitably causes discontentment and can lead to disgust with, and even to hatred of, ourself.

So, the question we each face is: **What is my truth, and how far am I willing to go to affirm it?** The response to this question defines who we really are and how we wish to live our lives. It merits close examination. And so long as your truth is not rooted in vice or injustice, I urge you to declare it loud and clear, with courage and determination. Because this affirmation, whatever its consequences, will be a source of unrivalled happiness and will allow you to live in harmony with your true self.

I AM WHAT I AM

———— Before affirming your truth, you must first accept it if we find ourselves trapped in a way of life that we consider to be the only respectable path, we may not accept our differences. This suffocation of one's truth most often manifests as confused thoughts and impressions of guilt: *I'm not normal for thinking that. I'm being ridiculous wanting to become an actor; it's not a serious career. I'm stupid for not liking football. How shameful it is to be gay.*

To avoid such spiralling thoughts and to rediscover the path of joy, there is only one solution: to accept one's truth. This means accepting that everyone has the right to be different, including you! It is to understand that the world is a mosaic in which every piece has its place and its own importance. Think of it like a football team, where each player has different qualities but every position is essential. We are all on the same team, and it is called planet Earth. ◆

TRUE LIES

Whatever our truth, it is vital to confront it; that is, to submit it to the tests of knowledge, debate and self-reflection. The more our opinions are examined and validated, the more they will be faithful to our inner self, and the more we will be in harmony with our true selves. But beware; some people will stop at nothing to ensure that their truth triumphs over ours. Fake news, lobbying, targeted marketing, political propaganda and even violence are all ways that allow people, businesses or states to impose their ideas, their products or their power. By operating at the frontiers of our free will, this 'army of darkness' manipulates our truth and therefore our happiness.

This sea of manipulation is strewn with broken lives. Take the example of the people of Germany who were manipulated by the propaganda of Adolf Hitler, and swept him to power in 1933, the consequences of which we are well aware. And also the members of the Order of the Solar Temple sect who, in 1995, committed suicide in Vercors, France, during a mass self-sacrifice intended to effectuate a 'transition' to the planet Sirius. Lastly, eight million smokers die worldwide each year because they have been manipulated by the powerful marketing of the tobacco industry[III]. So be vigilant and confront your truth. Have a thirst for knowledge, be open minded, but always know how to distinguish that which comes from within you from that which is guided by vested interests – your happiness depends on it. ◆

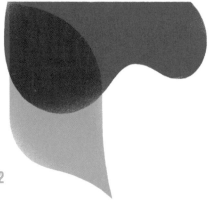

HAVE A THIRST
FOR KNOWLEDGE,
BE OPEN MINDED,
BUT ALWAYS KNOW HOW
TO DISCERN THAT WHICH
COMES FROM WITHIN
YOU FROM THAT WHICH
IS GUIDED BY VESTED
INTERESTS.

NOW

Write down your truths.

_____

_____

_____

_____

_____

_____

_____

_____

_____

_____

_____

_____

_____

_____

_____

_____

_____

_____

_____

_____

_____

_____

AFTER READING THE BOOK

*After taking time to confront your truths, declare them
loud and clear to those you care about most
(note their names down here).*

LIVING WITH *TRUTH* WILL HELP YOU TO BE HAPPY AND TO DEFINE YOUR DREAMS FROM A POSITION OF AUTHENTICITY. BUT WHATEVER THEY MAY BE, THESE DREAMS WILL HAVE NO VALUE UNLESS THEY ARE ACCOMPANIED BY AN EFFECTIVE *STRATEGY*.

STRATEGY

'All the success of an operation
lies in its preparation.'

– Sun Tzu –

BILLY

———— Its the close of the 2001 American baseball season, and Oakland Athletics are struggling. Its budget limited, the club sees its best players bought up by teams with greater resources, such as the New York Yankees. This situation hints at a difficult season to come for the team and for its manager, Billy Beane. Billy does not allow himself to be beaten. Obsessed with the dream of winning the championship title, he decides to adapt his strategy to handle his budgetary constraints. To do so, he calls on Paul DePodesta, a Harvard-trained economist. Together, they decide to revolutionise the recruitment process, by choosing players based only on their statistics (pitching success rate, batting average, etc.) and not their monetary value. They therefore decide to let go of a number of players who, until then, had been considered essential, and recruit cheaper players in their place. Many of these players had been rejected by other teams but their performance, in Billy and Paul's eyes, makes them invaluable.

The strategy is initially disappointing. Players, coaches, commentators and supporters deride Billy Beane, but he holds his ground and sticks to his strategy. Opinions soon change the following April, when Oakland Athletics begin to win one victory after another.

On 4 September 2002, Billy Beane and his team make baseball history by notching up their 20th consecutive victory, breaking the league record, which had until then been held by the New York Yankees. Oakland Athletics would end up at the top of the American League West and Beane would receive the accolade of Coach of the Year.

This true story, made famous by the film *Moneyball* (directed by Bennett Miller, 2011), reminds us that the pursuit of our goals requires implementation of a strategy that is adapted to our means and our environment. ◆

HAPPINESS THERAPY

It is very common to have a goal but never achieve it. It is not that we do not have the ability (deep down, this is very rarely the case) but quite simply that we do not manage to overcome the obstacles in our way: *There's not enough time! It's too difficult! It's too expensive!* The difficulties are multiple and often put an end to our most cherished dreams.

To spare ourselves these missed opportunities to achieve happiness, it is helpful to devise and apply a **life strategy**, meaning that we ensure that our actions correspond with the goals we wish to attain, which, according to several American researchers, is a contribution to wellbeing and satisfaction.

To be effective, this life strategy should be adapted to our environment (political affiliations, relationships, etc.) and our means (physical, intellectual, financial, etc.). This is how Billy Beane revolutionised baseball in 2002, and it is how you will revolutionise your life. Welcome to the Matrix ... ◆

MATRIX

We visualise it according to multiple parameters. Work, family, friends, admin, leisure and money are all inherent components of the lives of every, or almost every, human. These parameters are characterised by their interdependence, in that each is likely to have an effect on another. They can be classified according to five categories, which are also interconnected: human, operational, personal, external and spiritual.

HUMAN

Encompasses everything to do with your relationships, from your connections to your partner, family, friends, colleagues to all the strangers you happen to encounter (or do not).

EXTERNAL

Groups together all the aspects that influence our lives but are not dependent on us specifically – our employer, government, the environment, epidemics, the country we live in, etc.

PERSONAL

Concerns parameters that are partially dependent on us – health, sport, studies, work, hobbies, personal style, etc.

OPERATIONAL

Includes all the parameters associated with organising the practical details of your life, purchases to be made, transport, accommodation and administrative tasks.

SPIRITUAL

Is concerned with our relationship with religion, our political views and values and our philosophy of life.

A **life matrix** is determined by how these five categories are represented, with each of us populating them according to the parameters we consider to be essential to our lives. ◆

EXAMPLE :

HUMAN	OPERATIONAL	PERSONAL	EXTERNAL	SPIRITUAL
LOVE	HOME	HEALTH	BUSINESS	RELIGION
CHILDREN	TRANSPORT	STYLE	ENVIRONMENT	BELIEFS
PARENTS	MONEY	LEISURE	CITIZENSHIP	PHILOSOPHY
FRIENDS	ADMIN	WORK	PANDEMIC	POLITICAL AFFILIATIONS
	PURCHASES	SPORT		VALUES
	CHORES			

MATRIX RELOADED

To determine your life strategy, you need to consider each parameter of your matrix by applying the following four questions:

1. What is my current situation?

2. What is my goal?

3. How will I attain this goal?

4. What is the priority level for this goal? Three levels are possible:

Act now: my situation does not suit me and I have set myself a goal in order to change it; this goal is an absolute priority.

Maintain the status quo: my situation does not suit me and I have set myself a goal in order to change it; this goal is an absolute priority.

Act later: my situation regarding this parameter does not suit me; I have set myself a goal in order to change it, but this goal is not currently a priority because I have other goals to devote myself to first.

Let's take the example of Emily Gale[1], who is 36 and the editor of a sports-fashion magazine and website. Emily lives in San Francisco, and has been married to Peter for a year. She is passionate about cooking and surfing. Here are her answers to the four questions on page 45 for the parameters of work, environment and leisure:

PERSONAL

WORK

What is my current situation?
— I am the editor of a website and magazine dedicated to sports-fashion. Our sales have been declining for two years.

What is my goal?
— I want to find new revenue streams for the business.

How will I attain this goal?
— Having observed that streaming is really taking off in the United States, we are going to launch a sports-fashion TV channel that will be available on streaming platforms. The business shareholders are supporting this project, which they will finance with the investment of a new shareholder

What level of priority does this objective have today?

EXTERNAL

ENVIRONMENT

What is my current situation?

— I am very mindful of the need to protect our planet and of the dangers of climate change.

What is my goal?

— I would like to do my bit to help save the environment by signing up to volunteer with the *Surfrider Foundation*, an association that fights to protect oceans, lakes and rivers and the people that benefit from them.

How will I attain this goal?

— In a few months, as soon as I have finished setting-up our TV channel, I will sign-up at the San Francisco office, and I will set aside one Saturday every month to help the foundation.

What level of priority does this objective have today?

PERSONAL

LEISURE

What is my current situation?

— I have little time to devote to leisure, but it is vital for me to set aside some time for cooking and especially my cookery club. This regular meeting allows me to fulfil my passion, whilst also spending time with my best friends.

What is my goal?

— To continue to go to my cookery club every Wednesday evening, as I do currently.

How will I attain this goal?

— I must keep our Wednesday meet-up in my diary.

What level of priority does this objective have today?

Once this work has been completed for each parameter, this is what the matrix could look like for Emily, whose goals and priorities have been defined:

HUMAN	OPERATIONAL	PERSONAL	EXTERNAL	SPIRITUAL
LOVE	**HOME**	**HEALTH**	**BUSINESS**	**RELIGION**
Continue to keep the spark alive with Peter. ●	Continue to do up our house (odd jobs, decorating, garden, etc.) ●	Get a full check-up. ●	Continue to do my job well to retain the confidence of the shareholders. ●	Continue to go to Mass every Sunday. ●
CHILDREN		**STYLE**		**PHILOSOPHY**
Two years from now, Peter and I will try for our first child. ●	**TRANSPORT** Try out car sharing for getting to work. ●	Cut hair. ● Buy a new evening dress. ●	**ENVIRONMENT** Become a volunteer for the *Surfrider Foundation*. ●	Continue to treat life as a gift. ●
PARENTS Continue to see and call my parents regularly. ●	**CHORES** Washing, shopping, etc. every Friday. ●	**LEISURE** Keep our Wednesday cookery club meet-up going. ●	**CITIZENSHIP** Continue to go to vote at each election. ●	
FRIENDS Continue to see them often. ● Make up with Vick. ●	**MONEY** Renegotiate our mortgage. ● **PURCHASES** Replace the food processor. ●	**WORK** Launch a TV channel for streaming, alongside the magazine and website. ●	**PANDEMIC** Get vaccinated against COVID-19. ●	
COLLEAGUES Maintain the good atmosphere. ● Think about holding a seminar. ●	Buy an electric bike. ●	**SPORT** Surfing and running as normal. ●		

The secret to a good life strategy lies in our ability to prioritise our goals (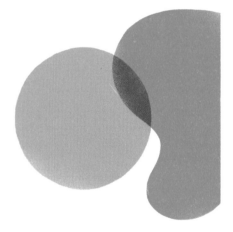) because, all too often, we want everything now and think all our goals take equal priority. The upshot? We do not find the time to meet all of our challenges properly, so burnout, haste and bad decisions can lead to disappointment . ◆

TIME IS ON MY SIDE

——— Once you have drawn up your life matrix, it is vital to plan accordingly. To do so, you will need to make space in your daily and weekly schedule for the actions you intend to take to fulfil or maintain the goals you have prioritised ( ). Here is Emily's diary for a typical week, as an example: ◆

	MON	TUES	WED	THURS	FRI	SAT	SUN
MORNING	**WORK** Team briefing	**WORK** Shareholder meeting	**WORK** Magazine editing	**WORK** Interviewing future recruits	**WORK** Shareholder meeting	**MONEY** Renegotiate mortgage **SPORT** Surfing	**RELIGION** Mass
AFTERNOON	**WORK** Website editing	**WORK** Accounts	**WORK** Present TV project to team	**FRIENDS** Lunch with Vick **WORK** Review of competitors	**WORK** Santa Monica fashion show **CHORES** Shopping, washing, self-care	**FRIENDS** Barbecue at home **PANDEMIC** Vaccination appointment	**PARENTS** Peter's parents visiting **PURCHASES** Food processor
EVENING	**LOVE** Quiet night in with Peter	**FAMILY** Cinema with my nephew and sister	**LEISURE** Cookery club	**COLLEAGUES** Dinner with partners	**PARENTS** Dinner at theirs	**LOVE** Restaurant with Peter	**SPORT** Running

DO NOT FALL INTO THE TRAP OF GIVING UP TOO EASILY: SHOW PERSEVERANCE IN ALL YOU UNDERTAKE.

MATRIX REVOLUTIONS

To summarise, a life strategy is implemented in three stages:

1. Draw up your life matrix and its parameters.

2. Apply the four questions on page 45 to each parameter of your matrix.

3. Integrate your goals into your schedule.

One last stage rounds off the process: facing up to reality. Once exposed to 'real life', some of your goals will turn out to be unrealistic to achieve. I recommend updating your life strategy every three months by re-applying each of the three steps detailed above.

These 'revelations' will help you to adapt better to your environment and be more effective. But be warned: it is often easier to give up on a goal than to strive to achieve it! Do not fall into the trap of giving up too easily; show perseverance in all you undertake – just as Billy Beane was able to in 2002. ◆

NOW

Write down the parameters of your life matrix
that you feel are most urgent.

_____

_____

_____

_____

_____

_____

_____

_____

_____

_____

_____

_____

_____

_____

_____

_____

_____

_____

_____

_____

_____

_____

AFTER READING THE BOOK

Draw up your life strategy following
the three stages outlined on page 53.

– The Seven Pillars of Happiness –

SETTING OUT A LIFE **STRATEGY** IS ESSENTIAL TO ATTAINING HAPPINESS. BUT TO BE EFFECTIVE, THIS STRATEGY SHOULD BE APPLIED WITH **LOVE**.

LOVE

'Love is the strongest force
the world possesses.'
Mahatma Gandhi

JFK

————— Launched in 1938 by researchers at Harvard University in the US, the *Study of Adult Development*[10] followed the daily lives of 724 men over almost 77 years[11]. What was the objective of this study? To find the secret to happiness.

Every two years, the Harvard researchers asked participants about their work, their family and their health. To complete their reports, they carried out blood tests and brain scans, as well as interviews with participants' families. The study panel were carefully chosen to include men from very different sociological backgrounds. Incidentally, John Fitzgerald Kennedy (JFK), the 35th president of the United States, took part in the study. The results of this scientific study, among the longest ever carried out, were made public in November 2015. The findings were definitive: the secret to a happy life lies in the quality of social relationships.

During the 77 years of research, the happiest men were those who had developed strong social connection (with friends, family, etc.). However, the most solitary of participants were the least happy. Interestingly, the study showed that it is not so much the number of social connections but the quality that is important[12].

This remarkable study, which is still ongoing, now includes women (it was about time). It does not specify whether JFK was a happy man, but it has taught us that love is the central pillar of happiness. ◆

THE KINDNESS OF OTHERS

At the heart of a relationship between two people is the way in which these individuals communicate. Without communication there is no relationship. We are often blinded by emotions, tiredness and life's hardships, and our words become hurtful. But it is impossible to cultivate love with hurtful words. Fortunately, there is kindness! Kindness is 'the quality of being friendly, generous and considerate'[13]. This notion can be found in many beliefs and religions, especially in Buddhism through the *bodhicitta*, which refers to the wisdom of love and compassion. The benefits of kindness are huge: for the person who receives it, of course, but also for the person who shows it! According to a number of studies[14], practising kindness promotes the secretion of oxytocin (a hormone that encourages empathy towards others), reduces stress, provides self-confidence and improves cooperation[15]. In concrete terms, practising kindness means treating others with benevolence and tolerance. ◆

He will then confide in you about his daughter's current health problems, which explain his frayed nerves. Perhaps even a friendly relationship will be born out of this exchange.

Or perhaps not. Because some individuals are too damaged and they will only respond with scorn or anger. Do not take offence. Persevere in your kindliness instead, because love attracts love. The trap we too often fall into is to respond to anger with anger, to violence with violence. We build walls rather than bridges. This reaction makes the situation worse and affects our wellbeing. Just one act of love can turn things around and reveal the face behind the mask; the face of someone who is wounded and simply needs to be loved. This is the essence of kindness; it is the bridge that links us with others. ◆

EXAMPLE:

The taxi driver who is taking you to the airport this morning did not greet you. He left you to put your own luggage into the car boot and complains endlessly about the traffic jams that fill your journey. Being kind in this instance could mean a sympathetic comment, such as 'Oh yes, it's true; it is difficult this morning, with all these traffic jams', or a thoughtful one: 'Well done for driving in all this traffic: it takes courage!'. Perhaps the driver will be touched by your kindly words.

WE ARE THE CHAMPIONS

It is very difficult to love others, to be kind to them, if we do not love ourselves. We live in a world where each life, each 'profile', seems perfect; a world where success is measured by the number of likes on social media; a world where there is no place for the weak, the poor or the anonymous. It is therefore very easy to find yourself 'wanting', to not love yourself – an underestimation of oneself that causes frustration and a loss of self-confidence. In 2003 Kristin Neff, a specialist in educational psychology at the University of Texas, highlighted and examined the notion of self-compassion[16]. The acclaimed researcher demonstrated that, in certain cultures, people are kinder towards themselves and, as a consequence, suffer less depression and frustration than in other cultures. This is the case in Thailand, where Buddhism promotes daily self-acceptance.

To be happy, then, Neff invites us to show kindness to ourselves. How? By focusing on our qualities rather than our faults; by choosing to contemplate what we have achieved rather than what we have not; and by thinking of the love that we receive, rather than that which we do not. ◆

———— Not everyone expresses their love in the same way. In his famous book, *The Five Love Languages*, Gary Chapman identifies five ways in which individuals tend to show their love: words of affirmation, quality time, gifts, acts of service and physical touch. Unfortunately, it is often the case that two people express their love via different languages when they interact, with unwanted consequences.

For example, if, in a romantic relationship, your language is words of affirmation, this means that you need your partner to compliment you or congratulate you often to fulfil your needs. You tend to pay a lot of compliments, because we always speak the language we would like to hear. However, if your partner's language is quality time, it is highly likely that your words of

THE LOVE LANGUAGES

affirmation will not have the desired effect and you will not be particularly inclined to make the effort to share quality time together. The upshot? Neither of you sees your need for love satisfied. The consequences over time are lack of understanding, frustration, insults, quarrels, separation and, ultimately, divorce.

This phenomenon of love languages applies to all relationships, whether romantic, friendly or professional. It is therefore vital to always try to recognise the language of the other person and then use it. How? By asking this person the right questions and by observing their words and their actions (the love language of someone who regularly gives gifts will very likely be gifts!). But first of all, don't forget to practise kindness, because this serves as the universal language of love. ◆

Life sometimes dishes out its fair share of unwarranted injustice and abuses. In the face of these wounds to the soul, only bitterness and anger survive, feelings that imprison us in a state of discontentment from which only love can deliver us.

FORGIVENESS

'Love is the strongest force the world possesses,' said Gandhi, and it is most nobly expressed through forgiveness. Whether you have been betrayed, ridiculed, robbed or assaulted, to aspire to happiness, you must forgive those who have hurt you.

The path to forgiveness is often long: when it is not the severity of the acts that we have been subjected to that prevents us from forgiving, it is our pride or our thirst for an impossible justice that crushes it. But if you can put yourself in the place of those who have hurt you, while accepting that everyone can fail (including you) forgiveness will appear. To facilitate this, it is necessary to look back on all the times when you, too, have failed and to accept that life's abuses can cause trauma in some of us; the consequences of which are violence, hate, racism, mental instability, etc.

Take inspiration from Noëlla Rouget, the French Resistance member who was deported to Ravensbrück concentration camp in 1944 and who, after the Liberation, requested a presidential pardon for the man responsible for her arrest and that of her fiancé, who was shot by the Germans.

At the end of the path, you will be rewarded because forgiveness delivers from anger and misfortune, and with it brings freedom and happiness. ◆

HELLO SUNSHINE

Gratitude means regarding the world around us with admiration. As far back as antiquity, Cicero[17] described gratitude as the mother of all virtues. Two thousand years later, scientists have demonstrated that this love of the world protects against stress and depression and promotes a positive outlook.

Practising gratitude is not an easy thing. Firstly, there are endless reasons for bemoaning life. Heartache, money problems, childhood trauma, gloomy weather, war, illness: all give us a reason to feel depressed. And, secondly, as neuroscience has proved, our brains more readily retain the negative aspects of our life than the positive.

As a consequence, numerous researchers[18] recommend keeping a **gratitude journal**, a sort of diary in which you describe the best moments of every day[19]. So, if you think you do not have the time to keep such a journal, make time!

In parallel with this gratitude homework, take time each day to notice the good in everything. Learn how to find joy in everything, or almost everything: while out running, take delight in your amazing capacity to move, rather than grumbling about the rain that is starting to fall. When one of your friends leaves, take the time to look back at all the good times spent together, rather than becoming sad at parting. At the office, savour exchanges with your colleagues, rather than complaining about your boss's frowning face.

But gratitude is also accepting life for what it is: for its most beautiful facets as well as the darkest. That is the sentiment that the famous poem by Mother Teresa encapsulates[20].

'Life is an opportunity, benefit from it.

Life is beauty, admire it.

Life is bliss, taste it.

Life is a dream, realise it.

Life is a challenge, meet it.

Life is a duty, complete it.

Life is a game, play it.

Life is costly, care for it.

Life is wealth, keep it.

Life is love, enjoy it.

Life is a mystery, know it.

Life is a promise, fulfil it.

Life is sorrow, overcome it.

Life is a song, sing it.

Life is a struggle, accept it.

Life is a tragedy, confront it.

Life is an adventure, dare it.

Life is luck, make it.

Life is too precious, do not destroy it.

Life is life, fight for it.'

– Mother Teresa –

NOW

Make a note of the three best moments of your day.

AFTER READING THE BOOK

Note down how you were kind towards yourself and others today. Who did you forgive, and what are you grateful for?

– The Seven Pillars of Happiness –

LOVE IS AN EXTRAORDINARY SOURCE OF HAPPINESS WHOSE FULL FORCE WILL ONLY BE REVEALED WHEN ONE'S *BODY* AND *MIND* ARE AT PEACE ...

BODY
& MIND

'We are not merely body nor merely mind;
we are body and mind all at once.'

– *George Sand* –

WALK OF LIFE

———— A few years ago, I set off from the town of Le Puy-en-Velay, in France, to walk the route that leads to Santiago de Compostela, in Spain. Over more than 65 days, I covered over 930 miles (1,500 km), at an average rate of 14 miles (23 km) per day. This adventure changed my life. I left with a heavy heart and returned a happy man, exalted by my recovered physique (I lost 1 stone/7 kg) and inhabited by a sense of wellbeing that has stayed with left me ever since.

Many things can explain this transformation. Among these is the fact that, since my return, I have not stopped walking: on average ten thousand steps per day. In 2012, researchers at the University of Stirling, in Scotland, highlighted the psychological benefits of walking, demonstrating in particular that it alleviates low mood, reduces negative thinking, helps stop rumination and promotes the regulation of emotions[21]. Likewise, in 2018, a study from Yale University[22], in the US, highlighted the beneficial effect of exercise on mood and mental health. To promote a feeling of happiness, the study recommended exercising for between 30 and 60 minutes three to five times a week[23].

Beyond these scientific studies, one thing is clear: using our minds and bodies can be incredibly beneficial for our mood. On the following pages you'll find an overview of the most widely recommended practices for setting us off on the road to happiness. ♦

BICYCLE RACE

COME TOGETHER

——— Cycling is the mode of transport that brings the greatest happiness! That is the conclusion of a recent study from the University of Minnesota, which studied the correlation between daily travel behaviour and emotional wellbeing[26]. Cycling helps us to achieve a temporary state of relaxation, thanks to the phenomenon of muscle relaxation associated with synchronisation of the breath and heartbeat, which can calm the mind. ◆

——— Walking is good for morale, but walking in a group may be even more beneficial, keeping depression at bay while also improving your social life[24]. This is highlighted by the studies of Dr Lisa Gorham, a specialist in cognitive neurosciences at the University of Washington. Dr Gorham has demonstrated that there is a link between participation in team sports and a lowering of the risk of developing depression[25] ◆

MOONLIGHT SWIM

In the race to happiness, swimming takes the lead. Being in water fosters a state of relaxation, subconsciously reminding us of our experience in utero. Further, the phenomenon of flotation, associated with Archimedes' principle[27], has qualities that are particularly relaxing, to such a degree that flotation therapy has become very popular. By combining the features of an aquatic environment with meditation techniques, being immersed in water can reduce stress and improve feelings of wellbeing. ◆

OPEN YOUR EYES

Living in and accepting the present moment is one of the keys to happiness. All too often our anxieties strip away our ability to enjoy the present moment. Mindfulness meditation is an effective way of combatting this.

Enshrined at the heart of Buddhist philosophy, this practice consists of focusing one's attention on the present moment by concentrating on the breathing and bodily sensations, and observing thoughts and emotions without trying to control them or pass judgement on them[28]. Mindfulness meditation leads to a recalibration of the brain that is both functional and structural, thanks to neuroplasticity[29]. It is used in hospital settings to relieve some psychiatric conditions, such as the management of stress, the prevention of depressive relapses, anxiety disorders and also addictions[30]. ◆

DEEP IMPACT

————— Originating in India, yoga is an ancient discipline that includes poses, breath control and meditation exercises. According to several studies, yoga reduces stress and improves mood[31]. A study from Boston University showed that 12 weeks of yoga helped reduce anxiety and increased levels of gamma-aminobutyric acid (GABA) in the brain[32] (low levels of GABA are associated with depression and anxiety disorders). ◆

LOL

————— The health benefits of laughter have been recognised since antiquity. Laughter ensures that blood is well oxygenated, as well as promoting good blood circulation, the secretion of endorphins and muscle relaxation. Laughter yoga[33] is a type of group therapy: people laugh intentionally, without relying on humour, and the laughter quickly becomes natural and contagious. In India, where the therapy was invented[34], this form of yoga is practised in many workplaces to reduce employee stress and increase wellbeing. ◆

LA LA LAND

Plato said of music that it finds its way 'into the secret places of the soul'. More than two thousand years later, this declaration takes on its full meaning according to recent scientific discoveries on the subject. Notably, it has been shown that certain musical frequencies resonate directly with our nervous system, thereby leading to a feeling of serenity and wellbeing. This appears to explain the calming effect of certain types of music, as the rhythms of the brain adapt to match those of the music. Gregorian chant is recommended for stress relief, baroque music for inducing a sense of calm and rock music for releasing inner tension[35]! ◆

Several studies highlight the influence of smell on our mood[36]. It is interesting that levels of phobia and depression are high in people with anosmia (loss of the sense of smell) [37]. Some scents are recommended for improving our mood, in particular:
- lavender to reduce anxiety and nervousness[38];
- lemon to improve self-confidence and feelings of optimism[39];
- ylang-ylang flower to lower blood pressure, reduce stress and combat depression by regulating the central nervous system[40];
- sweet scents, or 'gourmand fragrances', to promote feelings of reassurance [41]. ◆

PERFUME

RATATOUILLE

——— Our diet affects our mood! What we eat is absorbed into the nerve-cell membrane of our brain, which is mostly made up of fatty acids[42], and these fatty acids play an essential role in communication between the nerve cells in the body. One experiment has shown that, when omega-3 fatty acids were removed from their diet, the behaviour of laboratory rats changed within a few weeks; they became anxious, were panicked by the least stressful of situations and lacked any motivation to carry out new tasks.

Our food also has an impact on our gut microbiota, which is composed of the bacteria in the intestines. These bacteria secrete around 85 per cent of the neurotransmitters in the body linked to mood[43]. A team of French researchers has demonstrated the leading role that the microbiota plays in depression, underlining in particular the importance of taking prebiotics in balancing mood[44].

To attain or maintain a happy mood, it is vital to choose what we eat carefully. Countless studies [45] recommend one food or another to feed our mood, but the important thing is to choose foods rich in **omega-3** (such as salmon, anchovies, sardines, tuna, rapeseed oil, spinach and seaweed) and **prebiotics** (yoghurt, fermented vegetables, garlic, leek, asparagus and onion). ◆

TO MAINTAIN,
OR ATTAIN,
A HAPPY MOOD,
IT IS VITAL TO CHOOSE
WHAT WE EAT
CAREFULLY.

————— Blue light from the sun allows our body to secrete dopamine and serotonin, two mood-regulating neurotransmitters. This phenomenon explains the explosion in rates of depression in many northern-hemisphere countries during the winter, when sunlight is weaker. This 'seasonal depression' is characterised by considerable fatigue, a continuous

SUNSHINE

desire to sleep and increased sadness in the evening[46]. Fortunately, light therapy can help! Light therapy involves regular exposure[47] to a lamp that emits an intense white light[48], mimicking sunlight and compensating for the lack of natural light that causes seasonal depression. Another solution, more costly and less practical, is to depart for sunnier climes for the whole of winter. ◆

COLOUR OF NIGHT

Many practices can help to regulate melatonin and improve sleep quality, such as yoga, meditation, light therapy, exercise (although not after 6 pm) and diet. So, too, can certain essential oils and medication. If you have sleep problems, it is always advisable to contact a sleep specialist for advice as soon as possible. ◆

——————— Mood and sleep are closely linked. Sleep disturbance is often at the root of a low mood while, at the same time, stress and hyperactivity have an influence on the quality of our sleep. At the centre of this vicious circle is melatonin, a hormone produced naturally by the body and whose primary function is to balance biological rhythms.

NOW

Try a solo session of laughter yoga: laugh out loud for 3 minutes without stopping.

AFTER READING THE BOOK

*Rethink your lifestyle and your diet to promote happiness,
and note your priorities here.*

THERE IS NO QUESTION THAT WHEN YOUR **BODY** AND **MIND** ARE AT PEACE IT IS EASIER TO WALK THE PATH OF HAPPINESS, ESPECIALLY WHEN YOU ARE IN THE COMPANY OF **CONFIDENCE**.

CONFIDENCE

'If one advances confidently in the direction
of his dreams ... he will meet with a success
unexpected in common hours.'

Henry David Thoreau

PREDATOR

In certain situations, we humans become predators of our own happiness. Our perception of life departs from reality, and we display anxious behaviour and irrational thoughts: *This exam terrifies me; I'm never going to get my degree; I'll never find work*: *This virus will kill us all; if I go out, I'm sure my home will be burgled.* This thought process has a name: fear.

Sometimes useful and sometimes life-saving, fear, if not managed, can destroy feelings of happiness for some of us. Three fears prove especially harmful to us: fear of life, fear of death and fear of failure. These are poisonous fears, whose antidote is confidence. ◆

LIFE IS BEAUTIFUL

For the sociologist Frédéric Lenoir, humans are essentially on a quest for security: we are looking to survive rather than to live. Why? Because we are inhabited by the **fear of life**, which is fed by the trauma of our lives, from the smallest (a flat tyre, a fall from a bicycle, etc.) to the most serious (violent attacks, the death of loved ones, etc.). All of these blows undermine the confidence we have in life; they make us fear the unknown and we become prisoners of misfortune.

To overcome the fear of life, some are able to rely on their faith in a protective God. This confidence in a destiny guided by a benevolent hand can, for some people, lead to phenomenal strength, serenity and joy.

Beyond the spiritual path, there is another route: knowledge. Indeed, philosophy, science and history allow us to better understand our world and make it a little less frightening.

It is on knowledge that the most effective therapies for overcoming fear of flying are based. First by meeting the crew, to see 'behind the scenes', and then through a session on board a flight simulator, the goal is to make the mysterious environment represented by the plane ordinary, to make it familiar and therefore less terrifying.

Knowledge of 'real life' is also an effective remedy for the fear of life. Montaigne [48] said that travelling moulds the young. Nothing is more true: by experiencing all kinds of adventure, interacting with people from all walks of life and discovering different cultures, we are better able to understand the world and it therefore becomes a little less terrifying. ◆

THE SUM OF ALL FEARS

For the renowned American psychiatrist Elisabeth Kübler-Ross, there is a single fear concealed behind all our fears: the **fear of death**. She explains that, by peeling back any one of our fears, we will always end up reaching the fundamental fear underlying all others. To support her assertion, Kübler-Ross uses the example of someone who is petrified at the prospect of being given responsibility for a work project. By peeling back their fear, this individual will realise that they are prey to the fear of performing badly; underneath, they will discover the fear of being punished for failing, and then the fear of losing their job, and finally the fear of not being able to survive financially, then physically – that is to say, dying. According to Kübler-Ross, learning to free oneself from the fear of death is fundamental to being able to face all of our other fears. ◆

LIFE AFTER LIFE

the accounts of people who have 'come back to life' after experiencing brain death or clinical death[50] following an accident or a period in a coma.

To confront the **fear of death**, confidence in the existence of an afterlife is essential. The thought of dying ourselves, or losing a loved-one, is terrifying, and it's competely normal to fear this. However, believing in an afterlife undeniably lessens the anguish of death, especially when this is seen as somewhere magnificent: a paradise. This is entirely a question of religion, belief or personal conviction, and it is for each of us to explore individually. There is a scientific approach that explores death from the perspective of what happens after death: the study of near-death experiences, or NDEs. When we talk about NDEs, we refer to

It was Dr Raymond Moody, psychiatrist and Doctor of Philosophy at the University of Virginia, who was the first to carry out advanced studies in this area. His famous work *Life After Life*, published in 1975, shattered the certainty of millions of readers, and of himself. For his work, Dr Moody gathered and analysed hundreds of testimonies from people of different faiths who had experienced NDEs. These people had all 'come back to life' in full possession of their physical and mental capacities. Their testimonies can be summarised as follows:

WHEN THESE SURVIVORS 'COME BACK TO LIFE', THEY DESCRIBE BEING PROFOUNDLY CHANGED. THEIR EXPERIENCE HAS GIVEN THEM CONFIDENCE IN THE EXISTENCE OF AN AFTERLIFE.

People report that, on passing into a state of clinical or brain death, they left their physical body, and most were able to observe doctors at work resuscitating them, from the top of the room. Sometimes they relate extremely precise details: descriptions of surgical procedures, the actions of people present in adjoining rooms.

They then recount having travelled through a passage, often described as a tunnel, at the end of which a bright, comforting light awaited them, a light that some liken to a fully formed 'being'. They also describe, for the most part, having relived all the events of their life instantaneously.

Many also relate having met deceased loved ones, whose reassuring presence served to help them pass through the 'tunnel'.

When these survivors 'come back to life', they describe being profoundly changed. Their experience has given them confidence in the existence of an afterlife, which reassures them and releases them from the fear of death. This confidence makes their life more precious – and also happier. Finally, some people say that their experience has taught them that the purpose of life on earth is to learn to love. ◆

To overcome the fear of death, it is vital not to treat the subject as a taboo, as Dr Moody understood. Because to avoid death is to keep the 'mother of all fears' alive. Conversely, confronting this terrifying prospect with our beliefs or our faith, or by studying NDEs, can help us to make it less frightening and to make these words of Henry Miller's our own: 'I accept death as I accept life. It is an adventure.'

THINKING

To overcome the fear of failure and walk the path of happiness, the most advanced scientific studies and the shrewdest of arguments have nothing on Walter D. Wintle's classic poem 'Thinking', opposite:

If you think you are beaten, you are
If you think you dare not, you don't,
If you like to win, but you think you can't
It is almost certain you won't.

If you think you'll lose, you're lost
For out of the world we find,
Success begins with a fellow's will
It's all in the state of mind.

If you think you are outclassed, you are
You've got to think high to rise,
You've got to be sure of yourself before
You can ever win a prize.

Life's battles don't always go
To the stronger or faster man,
But soon or late the man who wins
Is the man who thinks he can!

– Walter D. Wintle –

NOW

*Make a note of three moments in your life
when you have felt these three fears (see page 82).*

AFTER READING THE BOOK

*Endeavour to make confidence your state of mind,
then make a note of all the situations you will
overcome thanks to confidence.*

NOW THAT THE END OF THIS BOOK IS DRAWING NEAR, THE TIME HAS COME TO CALL ON THE *SEVENTH PILLAR OF HAPPINESS*, THE ONE THAT WILL HELP YOU BE HAPPY IN ANY SITUATION ...

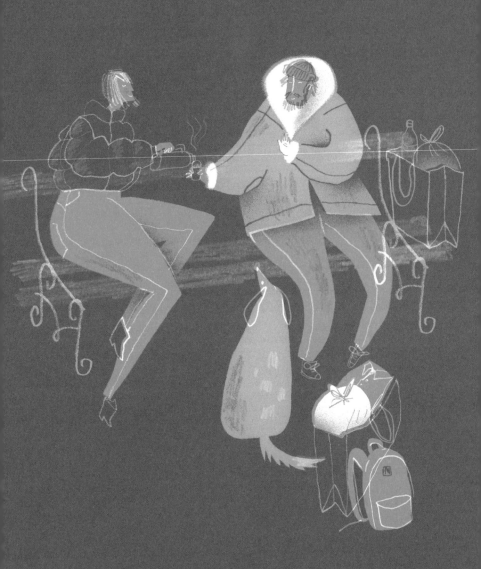

 # 04

Spend 30 minutes doing your favourite sport.

#05

Re-read the *Giving* chapter.

#06

Draw up or update your *Life Strategy*.

#07

Call three of your close friends and family and give them all your *Love*.

#08

Re-read *Super 8* eight times in a row.

#09

Make a list of the ten most important things that you would like to accomplish in your life.

#10

Laugh out loud continuously for 3 minutes.

#11

For 2 minutes, concentrate on thinking about those who are dearest to you and the love that you have for them.

#12

Re-read the chapter *Confidence*.

#13

Close your eyes for 2 minutes; do nothing, breathe deeply and think about all your qualities.

#14

Follow all the instructions, from #00 to #13.

STAY TUNED

Discuss, share, give feedback and discover the world of *41 Minutes to be Happy* and Géraud Guillet at www.geraudguillet.com and on social media.

SELECTIVE BIBLIOGRAPHY

Tal Ben-Shahar, *L'Apprentissage du bonheur*, Pocket, 2011. [English-language version: *Happier: Learn the Secrets to Daily Joy and Lasting Fulfillment*, McGraw-Hill, 2007].

Sonja Lyubomirsky, *Qu'est-ce qui nous rend vraiment heureux ?*, Les Arènes, 2014. [*The Myths of Happiness*, Penguin Publishing Group, 2014].

David Servan-Schreiber, *Guérir le stress, l'anxiété et la dépression sans médicament ni psychanalyse*, Pocket, 2011. [*Healing Without Freud or Prozac: Natural Approaches to Curing Stress, Anxiety and Depression*, Pan Macmillan, 2011].

Gary Chapman, *Les Langages de l'amour*, Farel, 2015. [*The Five Love Languages*, Moody Publishers, 2015].

Frédéric Lenoir, *Du bonheur, un voyage philosophique*, Le Livre de poche, 2015.

[*Happiness: A Philosopher's Guide*, Melville House, 2015].
Dr Raymond Moody, *La Vie après la vie*, J'ai lu, 2017. [*Life After Life*, Rider, 2001].

By the same author:
Géraud Guillet, ***L'Expérience TESK: à la fin de ce livre vous ne fumerez plus*** [*The TESK Experience: By the end of this book, you will have quit smoking*], Hachette Pratique, 2019.

FILMOGRAPHY

Moneyball, Bennett Miller, 2011
City of Joy, Roland Joffé, 1992

WEB SOURCES

TEDx – Study of Adult Development: https ://www.ted.com/talks/robert_waldinger_what_makes_a_good_life_lessons_from_the_longest_study_on_happiness ?language=en

TEDx – Study of Adult Development: www.ted.com/talks/robert_waldinger_what_makes_a_good_life_lessons_from_the_longest_study_on_happiness?language=en

Dr Kristin Neff – Self-Compassion: self-compassion.org

United Nations – International Day of Happiness: www.un.org/en/observances/happiness-day

World Health Organization: www.who.int/health-topics/depression#tab=tab_1

NOTES

[1] From poverty to street violence to the ravages of cyclones.

[2] By the General Assembly of the United Nations (UN).

[3] UN News, 20 March 2014: news.un.org/en/story/2014/03/464252

[4] WHO, 13 September 2021: www.who.int/news-room/fact-sheets/detail/depression

[5] CentraleSupélec. https://www.centralesupelec.fr/en

[6] TCC Montréal site (cognitive behavioural therapy): tccmontreal.files.wordpress.com/2015/01/laffirmation-de-soi.pdf

[7] Several studies highlight that expressing one's emotions, one's thoughts and one's opinions reduces stress and improves interpersonal relations.

[8] Géraud Guillet, *L'Expérience TESK: à la fin de ce livre vous ne fumerez plus* [*The TESK Experience: By the end of this book, you will have quit smoking*], Hachette Pratique, 2019.

[9] Fictional character.

[10] See the TEDx conference by Robert Waldinger, the fourth director of the study: www.ted.com/talks/robert_waldinger_what_makes_a_good_life_lessons_from_the_longest_study_on_happiness

[11] Harvard: www.adultdevelopmentstudy.org

[12] Those who experienced difficult relationships (divorce, quarrels or professional conflict) were found to be less happy than those who had enjoyed calmer relationships.

[13] Oxford Languages: www.lexico.com/definition/kindness

[14] Notably that of Dr Catherine Gueguen.

[15] The secretion of oxytocin is most often accompanied by the secretion of other hormones: endorphins (the happiness hormone), serotonin (a mood stabiliser) and dopamine (the hormone that gives pleasure to life, motivates and leads to creativity).

[16] Self-Compassion: self-compassion.org

[17] Cicero (106-43 BC) was a Roman statesman, a lawyer and a writer.

[18] Notably, Emmons and McCullough in 2003.

[19] All agree on the fact that, to enjoy its benefits, it is vital to practise gratitude regularly.

[20] Anjezë Gonxha Bojaxhiu, known as Mother Teresa, was a nun who received the Nobel Peace Prize in 1979. Born in 1910 in Kosovo, she became a nun in 1928 and later a missionary in India, where she died in 1997 in Calcutta. She was canonised by the Catholic Church as Saint Teresa of Calcutta on 4 September 2016.

[21] The study focused on 341 patients.

[22] Published by Professor Adam Chekroud.

[23] The explanation lies in the fact that exercise produces endorphins in our brain that reduce stress and cause a feeling of pleasure; it also promotes the growth of neurons and improves their functioning and their interconnection (mechanisms that are significantly impaired in depression and anxiety disorders).

[24] *Pleine Vie*, 16 June 2016: www.pleinevie.fr/sante/bien-vieillir/la-marche-cest-bon-pour-le-corps-et-le-mental-20179.html

[25] ResearchGate, January 2020: www.researchgate.net/publication/338824762_White_Matter_Tract_Integrity_Involvement_in_Sports_and_Depressive_Symptoms_in_Children

[26] www.cbsnews.com/minnesota/news/biking-happiness-commute-study-university-of-minnesota

[27] Any body that is immersed in a liquid undergoes an upward force from the liquid that is equal in intensity to the weight of the volume of liquid displaced.

[28] AFI Assurances: www.afiassurances.fr/magazine/mediter-les-bienfaits-sur-la-sante-le-mental-et-le-moral

[29] Studies of imaging performed on those who meditate have shown measurable changes in the regions of the brain associated with memory, attention, emotion and empathy.

[30] La Réponse du Psy: www.lareponsedupsy.info/Mindfulness

[31] National Library of Medicine: pubmed.ncbi.nlm.nih.gov/19701112

[32] *Science Daily*, 23 August 2010: www.sciencedaily.com/releases/2010/08/100819112124.htm

[33] *Hasya yoga*, in Sanskrit.

[34] By the Indian GP Madan Kataria and his wife, Madhuri Kataria.

[35] *Psychologies*, 19 March 2020: www.psychologies.com/Culture/Savoirs/Musique/Articles-et-dossiers/Musique-la-frequence-bien-etre

[36] Smell is the only sense that is not filtered by our consciousness, leading to physiological reactions that are independent of consciousness.

[37] *Le Temps*, 11 May 2017: www.letemps.ch/sciences/redecouverte-lodorat
38 *Passeport Santé*: www.passeportsante.net/fr/Solutions/PlantesSupplements/Fiche.aspx?doc=lavande_ps

[39] *So Busy Girls*, 2 December 2019: sobusygirls.fr/2019/12/02/parfum-huile-essentielle-citron-bienfaits-bonne-humeur-energie-optimisme-confiance-en-soi

[40] *Futura Santé*, 24 June 2019: www.futura-sciences.com/sante/questions-reponses/beaute-huile-essentielle-ylang-ylang-sont-vertus-4845

[41] Belle blog, 22 January 2020: www.carrementbelle.com/blog/fr/2020/01/22/pouvoir-du-parfum-influence-humeur

[42] David Servan-Schreiber, *Guérir le stress, l'anxiété et la dépression sans médicament ni psychanalyse* [*Healing Without Freud or Prozac: Natural Approaches to Curing Stress, Anxiety and Depression*], Pocket, 2011.

[43] Noradrenaline and serotonin.

[44] *Les Échos*, 'Dépression: c'est (beaucoup) dans le ventre que ça se passe' ['Depression: it's all in the stomach'], 22 January 2021.

[45] *Consumer Reports*, 20 August 2019: www.consumerreports.org/mental-health/what-you-eat-can-make-you-happier

[46] Dr Brigitte Blond, Doctissimo, 13 November 2019: www.doctissimo.fr/html/dossiers/luminotherapie/articles/11415-luminotherapie-contre-depression.htm

[47] Ideally, this should be practised on waking for 30 minutes every morning for five months.

[48] Without UVA or UVB, with an intensity of 10,000 lux.

[49] Michel de Montaigne (1533–92) is considered one of history's greatest philosophers.

[50] Absence of breathing and cardiac arrest for several seconds.

[51] France Générosités: www.francegenerosites.org/donner-bien-aux-autres-a-soi-meme

GIVING

'Everything that is not given is lost.'

– Mother Teresa –

ANNA

—————— Of all the testimonies that I have gathered, here is one that particularly moved me:

My name is Anna. I'm 28 years old and I'm a freelance journalist living in Paris. A few years ago, I suffered a severe episode of depression, despite nothing standing in the way of my happiness: I had a job that I enjoyed, a boyfriend who I loved, a caring family, and I hadn't experienced any particular traumatic in my childhood. In short, I had everything to be happy about. And yet I wasn't.

At that time, I always ended up spoiling each moment that could have been enjoyable. I fretted about everything, from the traffic jams on my journey and the weight that I was going to gain, to the fear of falling ill. I thought the world was against me and I blew the smallest of annoyances completely out of proportion. On top of this, there were long, bleak moments, during which I felt sad for hours at a time.

Everyone suffered from this situation; those close to me, of course, and me especially. After having consulted several doctors and tried multiple therapies without success, I began to despair of ever getting better. And yet it happened.

One winter's evening, my sister insisted that I
accompany her and several other volunteers on a soup
run in the streets of Paris. The idea was to distribute
food and hot drinks to homeless people while taking
the time to chat with them. Without really knowing
why, I decided to try it.

That night, I discovered a world that I had been
unaware of; that of the poor and the marginalised. I
came across these people every day on the way to work,
without really seeing them. Or rather, without wanting
to see them. As the night wore on, I became more aware
of the misery that life deals to some: theft, poverty,
illness, acts of violence; these broken souls seemed to
have been spared nothing. However, paradoxically,
this outpouring of suffering didn't get me down. On
the contrary, it gave me strength! So, each time that we
came to the aid of a homeless person, I surprised
myself by talking to them, comforting them, without
fatigue ever overshadowing my remarkable night.

In the early hours, despite the lack of sleep, I felt
unbelievably good. Something had changed within me.

At the time, I couldn't explain it. Today, I have come to understand that, that night, I had done something that I hadn't managed to do for a long time: I had forgotten myself. I had put my ego, my own interests, to one side and allowed myself to be moved by the suffering of strangers. And that had made me happy. My many 'problems' no longer weighed so heavily on me in the face of the joy of helping these people by giving them a little of my time.

Afterwards, I carried on accompanying my sister on these soup runs. I also got involved in other organisations and in other causes, continuing to find extraordinary joy in giving a little of myself to those in need. Since that night, I have never gone back to feeling sad. ◆

CITY OF JOY

————— Anna's story illustrates what scientific studies[51] have demonstrated; that is, that selfless giving:
— promotes a sense of wellbeing by releasing endorphins;
— improves resistance to stress and boosts the immune system;
— causes pleasure by stimulating the areas of the brain associated with the reward system;
— increases self-esteem, the sense of being connected with others and the feeling of making an impact. ◆

GIVE A LITTLE BIT

————— Giving can take many forms, but they all bring joy:
Give your time. Give your money. Give your friendship. Give a smile. Give thanks. Give your talent. Give your forgiveness. Give encouragement. Give blood. Give a hug. Give your heart. Give advice. Give your trust. Give your nights. Give your food. Give your love. Give life. ◆

NOW

Note down the three most beautiful gifts that you have been given during your life.

AFTER READING THE BOOK

*Get involved in one or several causes that are close
to your heart and write down the details here.*

YOU ARE NOW READY TO COMBAT SADNESS AND DESPAIR BY EMPLOYING THESE SEVEN EXTRAORDINARY RESOURCES: MEANING, TRUTH, STRATEGY, LOVE, BODY AND MIND, CONFIDENCE AND GIVING.

HAS LIFE LEFT YOU FEELING LOST AND HOPELESS? GIVE *MEANING* TO YOUR LIFE: MAKE YOUR LIST!

DO YOU FEEL AT ODDS WITH THE LIFE YOU LEAD? MAKE SURE THAT YOU ARE REALLY LIVING ACCORDING TO YOUR *TRUTH*.

ARE YOU UNABLE TO REALISE YOUR DREAMS?
GIVE YOURSELF THE TOOLS TO SUCCEED:
CREATE YOUR MATRIX AND DEVISE
YOUR LIFE *STRATEGY*.

ARE YOU FRETTING ABOUT A RECENT
ARGUMENT WITH YOUR BEST FRIEND?
USE *LOVE* TO FORGIVE THEM!

ARE YOU FEELING DOWN? USE YOUR
BODY AND YOUR *MIND* WISELY!

ARE YOU AFRAID OF EVERYTHING AND IT IS
RUINING YOUR LIFE? MAKE *CONFIDENCE*
YOUR STATE OF MIND.

ARE YOU FEELING BLEAK AND UNABLE TO
THINK OF ANYTHING BUT YOUR PROBLEMS?
GIVE A LITTLE OF YOURSELF TO SOMEONE
IN NEED.

AND IF ALL THAT DID NOT DO THE TRICK,
RE-READ THIS BOOK CHAPTER BY CHAPTER
OR ALL AT ONCE. OR ELSE READ *SUPER 8*
AND PLAY *THE GAME*
(SEE PAGE 119).

NOW

"I am the master of my fate;
I am the captain of my soul."
—William Ernest Henley

NOW OR NEVER

———— By now, you will not only be aware of the obstacles that lie in the way of your happiness, but also of the pillars that will help you to overcome them. It is these pillars that have helped me live as a happy man, that have allowed Paul and Anna, who we met earlier in the book, to rediscover the joy of life. These pillars also allowed Billy Beane to realise his dream and become a base-ball legend. And these pillars will help you to find the path of happiness, and perhaps much more besides.

You are the captain of your soul. Your friends and family are the passengers in your life. It is time for you to decide to be happy, for you and for them. You have complete freedom, and your choice is simple: change nothing or take your destiny in your hands by making the seven pillars of happiness the cornerstones of your life.

If this is your choice, I highly recommend that you fix this moment in your mind, because it will act as a beacon to which you can turn to at times of sadness and distress. It will remind you of all that now underpins your life: these seven indestructible pillars that should not be relinquished for anything. So make your decision now! ◆

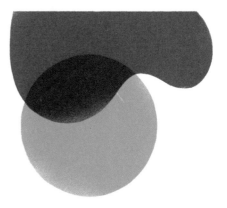

ALWAYS

———— Never forget that the seven pillars of happiness are there to support you throughout your life, because life's cruelty can catch up with us at any time. That is why you should always keep this book close to hand, to dip back into as circumstances demand. That way, you will avoid straying from the path of happiness. ◆

SUPER 8

———— If you only take **eight things** away from this book, remember the following:

01
What is important is not reaching the end of the path but walking the right path.

02
Living truthfully allows you to live happily.

03
Fulfilling any objective requires a strategy.

04
Love is the most powerful force in the universe and the central pillar of happiness.

05
The body and mind are vehicles of happiness.

06
Confidence annihilates fear.

07
Giving, without expecting anything in return, brings joy.

08
Happiness can be attained at any age. ◆

THE GAME

———— To play *The Game*, nothing could be simpler.
When you feel sad, anxious or angry:
— Look at the time.
— Add together the minute figures for that time.
— Follow the instructions for the corresponding
  number.

Example: The time is 10.29
— Add 2 + 9: you will get 11.
— Follow instructions for #11.
Further example: It is 07.10
— Add 1 + 0: you will get 1.
— Follow the instructions for #01.

00
Look back over the three best moments of your day.
01
Close your eyes and do nothing for two minutes.
Breathe deeply and think of all the beautiful things
you have accomplished in your life.
02
Re-read the *Truth* chapter.
03
Give something that is precious to you to someone
for whom that item will have value.